The Experience Book

21 Days of Beautiful Experiences from the Angels

Sue Broome

The Experience Book

21 Days of Beautiful Experiences from the Angels

Copyright © 2019 Sue Broome

Available from Amazon.com and other retail outlets.
Available on Kindle and other devices.

Cover design by Kim Richardson
mybizprovider.com
Cover Photo Credit:
A_Different_Perspective @ Pixabay.com

Mandalas created by Sue Broome.

ISBN: 978-0-9891879-2-3
ISBN-13: 978-0-9891879-2-3

The Experience Book

DEDICATION

I dedicate this book to you, the reader. I have a love for Angels and what they have shared with me over the years. The experiences they have shared with me bring me joy and many times are exactly what I needed to hear. I wanted to share these beautiful experiences with you as they may be exactly what you needed as well.

Table of Contents

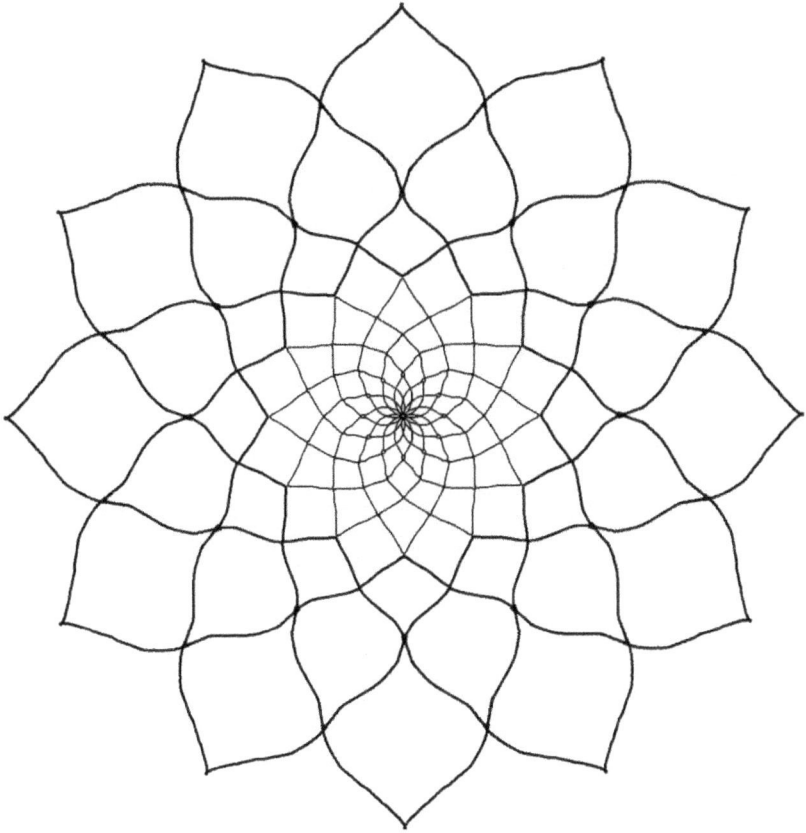

Introduction

Every week I settle in to write Monday's blog. I ask the Angels what they would like to share this week. Sometimes they will give me something immediately, other times it is something that has been going on in my day or week that I will share first, and then the Angels will bring their words of wisdom, for me and for you.

Some weeks it is not something they will necessarily share in words. They want me to write about an experience. It may come through as I am experiencing it, I am also writing what they are asking me to do. Other times I will write about it and then go through and experience what I wrote.

No matter how I get the information, the Angels have amazing and wonderful experiences to help us in our lives. All we need to do is stop and allow ourselves to experience what the Angels are sharing with us. They truly are experiences the Angels would like us to have for ourselves.

The Angels wanted me to pull these experiential blogs together and offer them as something you could do each day. They kept nudging until I sat down and started working on this little book with wonderful things to experience.

The Angels want us to know these experiences will benefit us when we take the time for ourselves. They will help our lives be happier and filled with more joy and love. They will transport us out of what may be happening in our day to day life and look at whatever is coming up in our day, from a higher perspective, a more loving and objective point of view.

The Angels also like to remind us, to feel the love they have for us. They want us to feel this, to experience this, much more often and on a much larger scale. This is what will continue to help us evolve and grow, not only as individuals, but as a global consciousness as well.

I would encourage you to read through and experience, one of these every day. You could do a different one each day or pick one of them and choose to do it for several days or even a week at a time.

There are other ways to choose:

• Go through them in order, from beginning to end, and then start over.

• Fan through the pages and pick whichever one your fingers fall upon.

• Ask the Angels to pick one for you.

You may notice there are 21 days of experiences. The Angels wanted to keep the number 21. They feel 21 is a powerful number and that it would instill a habit if you are to do one every day for 21 days.

Their intention with this book is to help each of us, you and me, to raise our vibration every day, feel more love in our lives each day and to expand and grow. Their intention is for us to feel how powerful we are and that each of us, can make a difference, in our own lives as well as in raising the vibration of the planet.

As you go through each day, you may want to have a journal handy to jot down any thoughts or ideas that come to you. Each experience may bring some things to the surface you were unaware was even there.

The Angels are here to support us, in all we do. All we need do is ask.

Further along in the creation process of this book, the Angels decided to add a mandala, sometimes multiples, for each of the experiences. I discovered a wonderful application where I was able to create all of the mandalas myself.

The Angels intention with the mandalas is for you to either gaze upon them at the beginning of your going through the experience, to color them if you would like or to meditate with the mandala itself. Whatever you choose to do with the mandalas, is right for you.

There are 21 experiences, although there may be multiple mandalas for some of the experiences. If there are multiple feelings or emotions from following through the process of the experience, I was guided to do a mandala for the experience as a whole as well as the individual feelings or emotions.

There may be some mandalas for the same feeling, though because of the rest of the experience, an additional mandala was created.

There are healing properties with each mandala, which is amplified the more you work with the experience.

The mandalas are also available to print, on my website.

The mandalas are also available to print, on my website. The page is: http://bit.ly/TEBMandalas with password being **Mandalas**.

Angel Blessings to you.

Sue

The Experience Book

Experience

Your

Angelic

Team

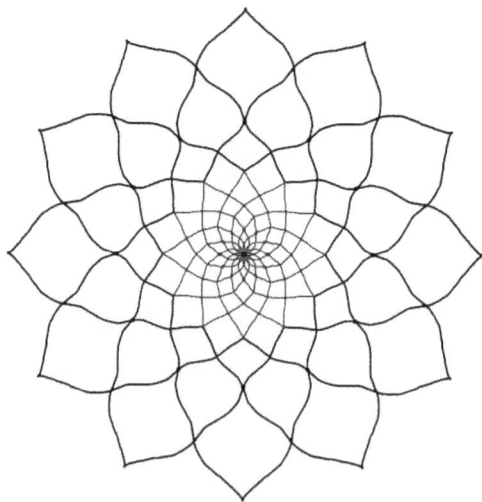

Dear Ones,

You are worthy. You are deserving. You are valuable. You are a shining light. You are a blessing. You are a gift. You are beautiful. You are loved.

You are a spiritual being having a human experience and you have worthwhile things to share.

We are your cheering section. We are your Angelic Team, here to assist whenever you need:

- *A boost*

- *Some help*

- *Inspiration*

- *Encouragement*

- *Healing*

- *Just the right words for any given situation*

- *Protection*

What do you need right now, today? Ask and we will be there.

~ Your Angels ~

Sue Broome

open to experience

Sue Broome

angelic team

Sue Broome

Experience

Peace

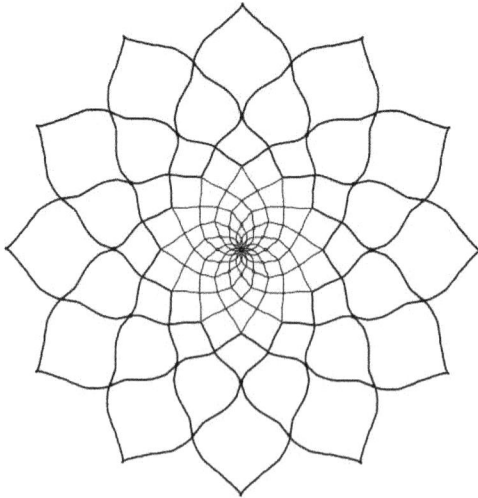

Dear Ones,

This is two-fold, the peace within and the peace around you. The peace within is where you start. Watch it spread to those around you, your space around you, the more you practice the peace within.

- *Sit and close your eyes.*

- *Notice your breath — don't change it, just pay attention.*

- *Feel the rhythm of your breathing, in and out and in and out.*

- *Notice how your body moves with your breathing.*

- *Imagine there is nothing else, anywhere, except your breathing. The whole world is your breathing.*

- *Imagine with each breath, you are breathing in peace and breathing out peace. Imagine and watch the space you are in shift to peace.*

- *Expand the peace you are breathing out to extend beyond your room, your home, your city, your county, your state and beyond.*

- *Imagine your peaceful breath combining and expanding even more with all the others who are doing the same.*

- *Come back to you, come back to the peace within.*

Repeat one or all of these, over and over in your mind or speak them out loud over and over, throughout your day.

- *Peace*

- *I am peace*

- *I allow peace in my life*

- *I allow peace to fill my every cell*

No matter what is going on around you, you can choose the peace within. You can choose to extend and expand the peace. We are happy to assist, all you need do is ask.

~ Your Angels ~

peace

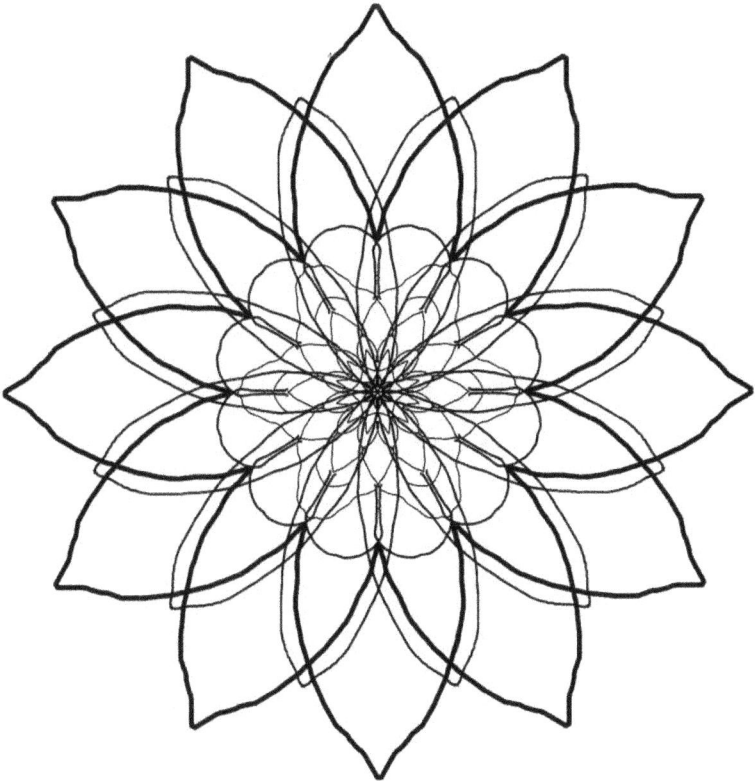

Sue Broome

Experience

Love,

Peace,

Calm

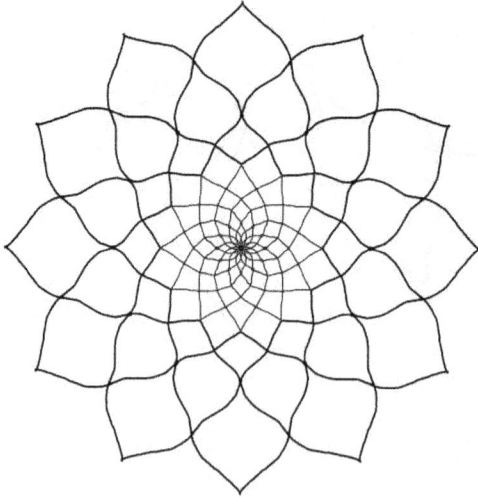

Dear Ones,

Imagine you are in the most beautiful garden. This garden has more colors and fragrances then you have ever experienced or seen before.

You are sitting quietly on a bench in the garden. You can smell the aroma of many different flowers, some you are familiar with and many you are not.

As you are sitting there relaxing with your eyes closed, and you notice there is a warmth on the top of your head. It feels like your head is buzzing a bit as well. It feels good, and you know this is a positive and wonderful experience.

You allow the buzzing and the warmth to soak into your body. You know on many levels it is healing what may have recently come to the surface.

You soak it up until it slowly subsides.

You are left with a wonderful sense of love, peace, calm and bliss.

~ Your Angels ~

Sue Broome

love, peace, calm

Sue Broome

love

Sue Broome

peace

Sue Broome

calm

Sue Broome

Experience

Love,

Peace,

Harmony

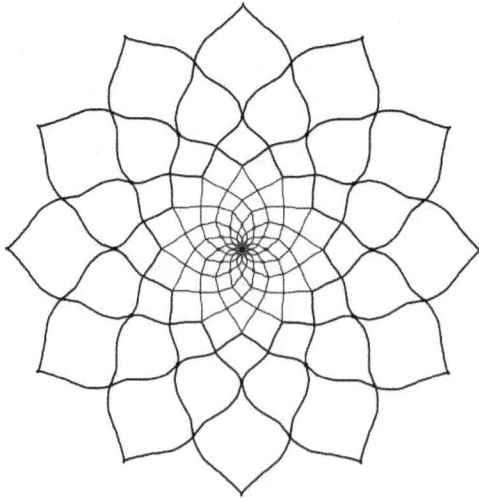

Dear Ones,

We want you to experience — love, peace, harmony, grace, compassion, softness, ease, flow — you get the idea!

There has been so much going on in the world that has many of you feeling anxiety or apprehension. There is so much growth and expansion you are going through. That is what some of it is as well. It's a feeling you have not necessarily felt in a long time.

Some is due to the changes and evolutions going on around you. It may affect you directly and even if it doesn't appear to, it does affect you as all are connected.

Please do this at least once a day and especially whenever you feel anxiety coming on:

Breathe

- *Feel your intake breath come in through your nose and expand into your cells*

- *Breathe so you can feel this life-force come all the way down to your very toes*

- *Hold for just a couple of seconds*

Exhale

- *Release through your mouth*

- *Let go of any tensions carried in your body*

- *Allow fears to fall away*

Feel

- *Love and peace within you*

- *Our loving wings enveloping you with love, compassion, peace, joy, harmony*

Allow the Divine energy

- *To fill every cell of your being*

- *To melt through your body, head to toe, filling every single space*

- *To move through you, deep down into Mother Earth, connecting our love, your love and Mother Earth's love, even stronger*

We love you and are here to help you feel more love, peace, harmony and ease.

~ Your Angels ~

love, peace, harmony

Sue Broome

love

Sue Broome

peace

Sue Broome

harmony

Sue Broome

Experience

the

Stars

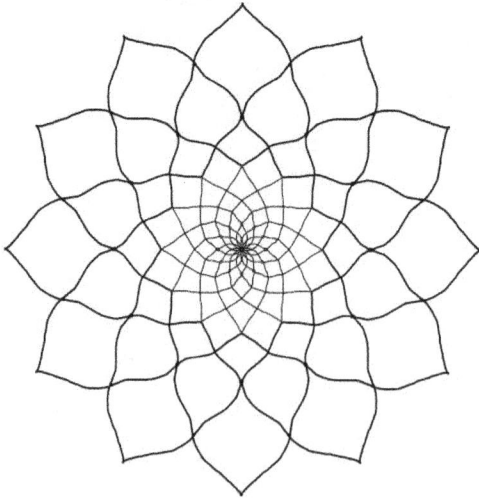

Dear Ones,

Today we would like you to have an experience with us.

- *Sit quietly and close your eyes.*

- *Breathe in and out several times to release any tensions you are holding in your body as well as breathe in the loving connection to all things.*

- *Imagine all the stars you've ever seen in front of you and surrounding you with the open expanse of space.*

- *You can sense you are moving forward, slowly, as it looks like you are passing some of the stars as you move through space.*

- *There is nothing you need do, just observe as you move slowly through the stars.*

- *As you move past them you notice there is an energy that connects with your inner knowing.*

- *There is nothing to do ... just be, observe.*

- *Allow yourself to be in this state as long as you would like.*

- *When you are ready, connect with Mother Earth, wiggle your hands and toes and open your eyes.*

You may want to journal after this experience. It will be different for each of you, and it will be different each time you do it.

We are here for you, all you need do is ask.

~ Your Angels ~

Sue Broome

the stars

Sue Broome

Experience

Looking

Beyond

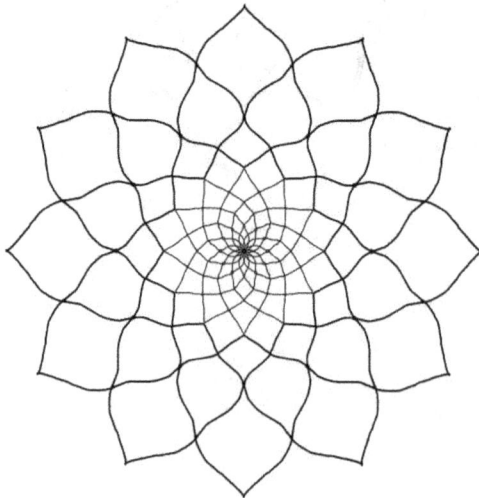

Dear Ones,

We would like to give you an experience that will assist you with looking beyond.

To start this experience, think of a situation. Whether the situation is a person, place or thing makes no difference. Have the situation come to your mind and then write it on a piece of paper, summed up in just a few words. Then set the paper down and do the following:

- *Close your eyes.*

- *Take several deep breaths in through your nose and out through your mouth.*

- *Bring in unconditional love from the Divine, from Mother Earth and mix with your unconditional love. (You may want to remember someone you love.)*

- *Feel this love in every cell of your being, flowing and filling each cell to the brim.*

- *Notice a smile coming to your face, still feeling this love.*

- *Now pick up the piece of paper and hold it between both of your hands.*

- *Continue feeling the unconditional love, continue feeling the love of the Divine and Mother Earth flowing within.*

- *Now remember what you wrote on the piece of paper, continue feeling the unconditional love flowing.*

- *Feel the love flowing to the situation on the paper and continue feeling the unconditional love.*

- *Hold this as long as you feel comfortable.*

- *When you are ready, open your eyes.*

When you are finished with this experience, please add the word "love" to the paper and place it someplace where you will see it often. Each time you see the note, think of the love and send it to the situation.

Watch to see how the situation changes over the next few days. Continue sending love, looking beyond the situation at hand, seeing just the love.

~ Your Angels ~

looking beyond

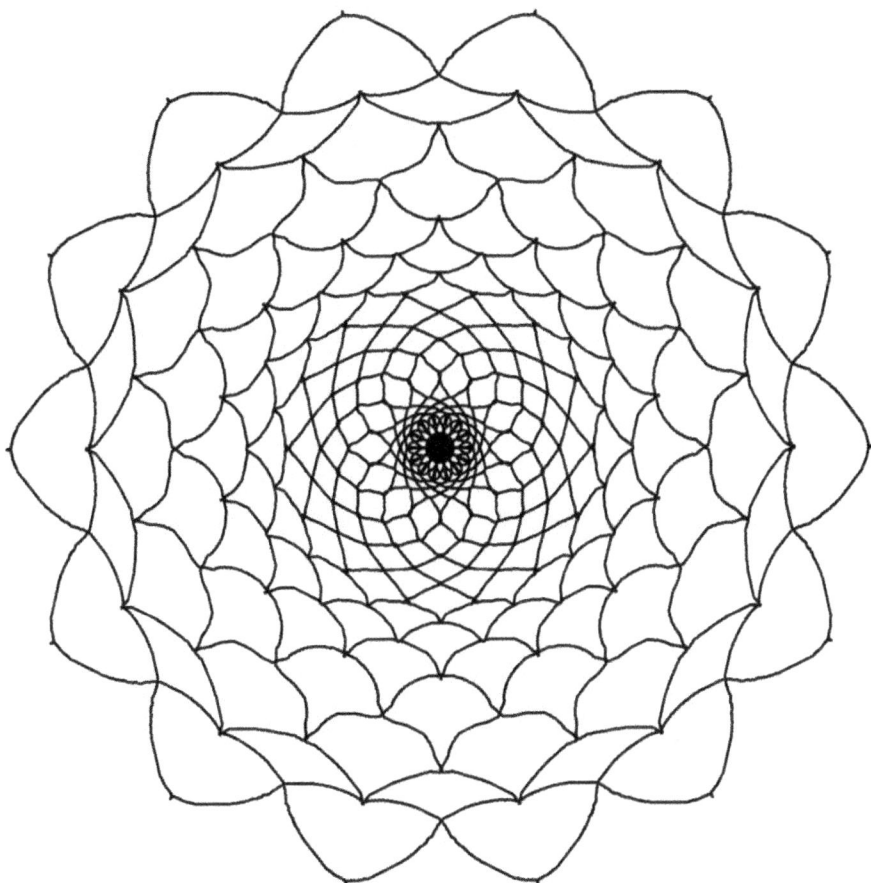

Experience

Ease

and

Grace

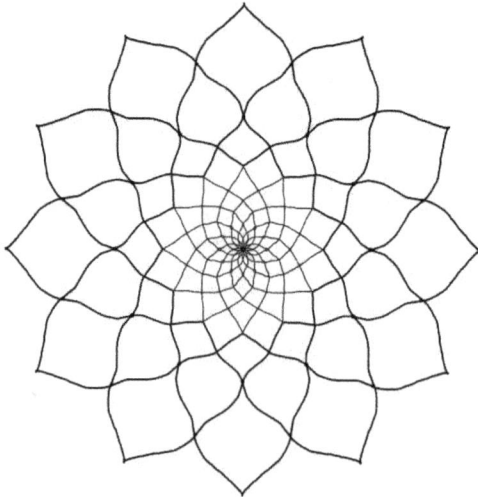

Dear Ones,

There is a soft flow to the universe that you can easily tap into. When you are in this soft flow, you notice the ease and grace. In fact, when you are in the space of ease and grace you are the soft flow.

You may be thinking your life is anything but ease and grace.

It is there, you just need to get there. Once you are there, it comes much easier each time, and soon you will be there and the other will seem like it was long ago.

A short experience of ease and grace:

- *Sit in a quiet location and take several deep breaths (closing your eyes is up to you.)*

- *Imagine there is a river in front of you. Notice the water is slowly moving. You almost have to look closer to tell that it is moving. You notice the water gently bubbling in some areas and yet it just continues to move.*

- *You're sitting on the land, just watching and noticing the movement.*

- *As you watch, more things fall away from your mind and you are only focusing on the slight movement of the water.*

- *You may notice a fish jump in the water, almost silently, creating a small ripple which quickly dissipates.*

- *You notice your breathing has slowed. You notice there is no tension in your body, like it has been washed away with the river.*

- *Ease and grace, soft flow.*

- *When you are ready, you can come back to your day.*

This is something that only takes a few moments and you will feel how your day shifts. When something isn't going with the soft flow of ease and grace, take a moment and watch the gentle flow of the river and see if "that something" changes with it.

Sue Broome

~ Your Angels ~

ease and grace

Sue Broome

ease

Sue Broome

grace

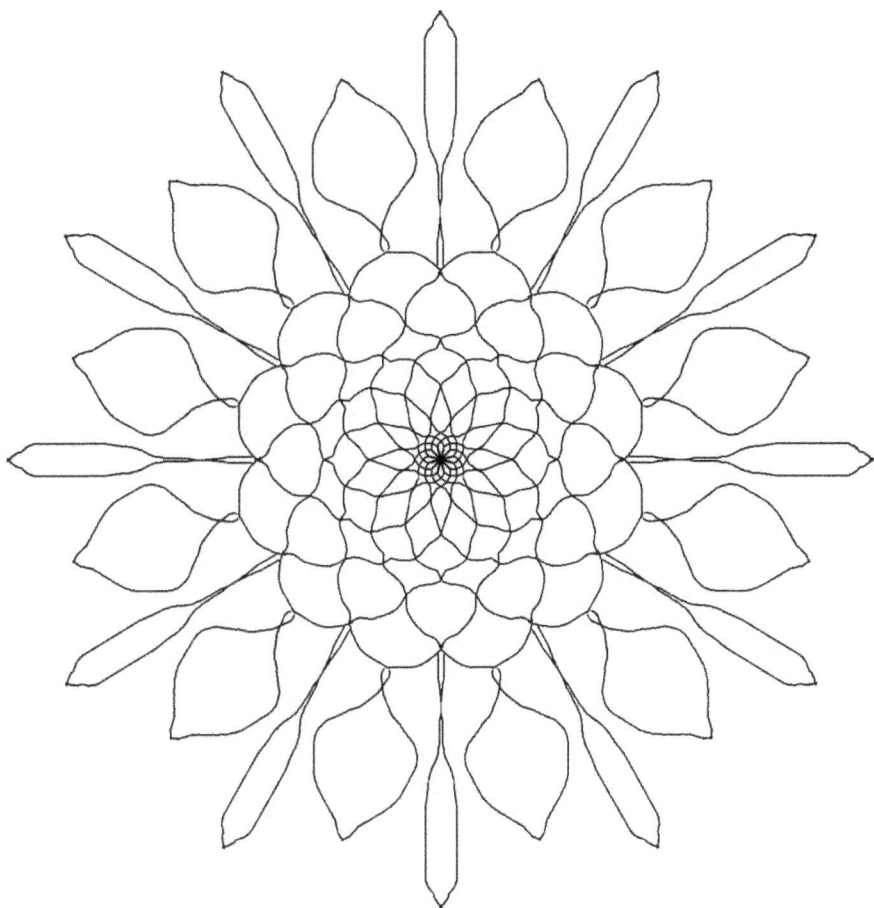

Sue Broome

Experience

Connection

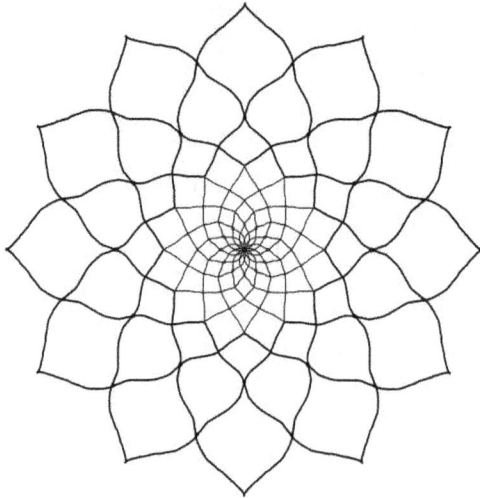

Dear Ones,

We see there are many who feel alone or feel as though there is no one to turn to in a time of need. You feel as though there is no one you would like to share a thought or an experience with, that you just had.

With so many people in your world, on your earth, there are still so many who feel alone.

We want you to know we are here for you, always. We listen to all you have to say and we love you.

Come with us on this journey:

- *Close your eyes and take a couple of deep breaths.*

- *Imagine you are sitting in a beautiful garden that feels sacred and inviting.*

- *You are sitting on a bench near many flowers of all different colors. You are feeling totally relaxed. The bench is very comfortable.*

- *As you are sitting there, taking in the wonderful scents of the flowers and feeling the soft breeze on your face, you are also noticing the vibrancy of all the colors around you.*

- *Then you realize there is someone sitting next to you on the bench – an Angel.*

- *You feel a protective bubble has formed around the two of you, though there is nothing to see, just the feeling. You feel so safe, so loved.*

- *You can tell this Angel anything, anything about your day, about your life, about what is going well, about what isn't going so well, about your hopes and dreams. They hear you, they see the true you. They listen.*

- *There is a feeling of love like you have never known before wash over you and stay with you.*

- *You feel heard, you feel loved, you feel safe.*

- *The Angel will stay as long as you would like. You can share anything you want.*

- *Ask the Angel any questions you would like as well.*

Your Guardian Angels will do this with you for they are with you throughout your lifetime. There are many others of us who are happy to sit on the bench with you, listen to whatever it is you'd like to share and happy to offer any assistance you would like.

We are here for you, we love you and we love having conversations with you. We want you to feel the love we have for you.

~ Your Angels ~

connection

Sue Broome

Experience

Being

Centered

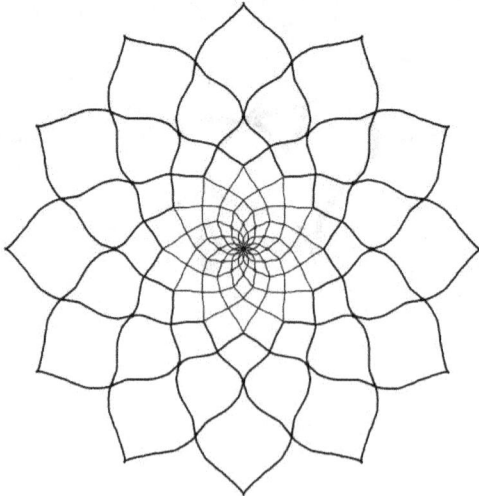

Dear Ones,

Today we would like you to experience feeling centered.

- *Find a location where you will not have any interruptions.*

- *Sit down and get yourself very comfortable, closing your eyes.*

- *Take several deep breaths, relaxing more and more with each breath.*

- *Imagine you are on a floatation device, floating on the water.*

- *You can feel the water moving gently beneath you.*

- *The sun feels wonderfully warm on you.*

- *There is a soft breeze blowing.*

- *There is nothing you need to do, nothing you need to think about.*

- *You feel as if you are receiving a gentle massage as you are just floating there.*

- *Thoughts come in and thoughts go out.*

- *All tension falls away.*

- *Lay there as long as you would like.*

- *Take a couple of deep grounding breaths, imagining now you have tree roots growing out of your feet, going deep into Mother Earth.*

- *Open your eyes when you are ready.*

We know in your life, experiences like this are so beneficial to you. They allow you to get centered again, having stresses wash away. You feel more energized and more like yourself afterwards. Ideas and inspiration are more likely to come to you when you are feeling refreshed.

Enjoy the experience.

~ Your Angels ~

Sue Broome

being centered

Experience Feeling Loved and Filled with Joy

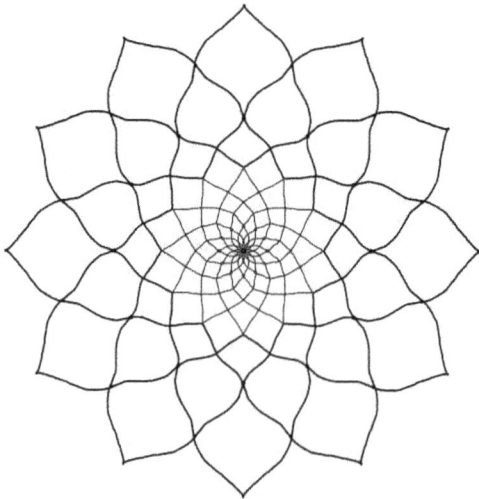

Dear Ones,

Today we want you to have an experience.

- *Find a quiet location and sit down.*

- *Close your eyes and take a couple of deep breaths.*

- *Allow your stresses to wash away.*

- *Imagine that you are looking up to the sky.*

- *Imagine all of the colors of the rainbow as flakes falling from the sky.*

- *Imagine that every flake is so beautiful and vibrant, filled with love.*

- *The colors are falling and swirling all around you.*

- *You feel loved, you feel vibrant, you are filled with joy.*

- *Open your eyes whenever you are ready.*

We love you.

~ Your Angels ~

Sue Broome

feeling loved

Sue Broome

filled with joy

Sue Broome

joy

Sue Broome

Experience

the

Connection

with a

Loved One

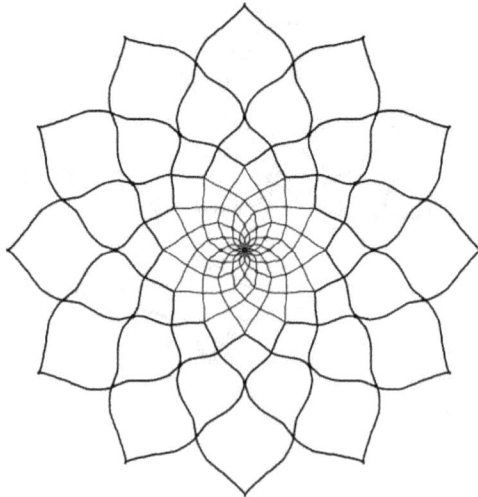

Dear Ones,

This is a message for anyone missing another. It does not matter if the person is in spirit or still in their physical body and just away from you for whatever reason. It is still a feeling you feel within your body and there may be emotions that decide to share themselves. Allow your emotions to flow when they decide to show themselves.

Choose one of your favorite memories and recreate it. Recreate it with your mind, with your imagination. Recreate a memory that has so much meaning to you and your loved one.

Let them know when you will be doing this and set it up. It's a date! You can tell them, write a note, add it to your calendar, think about it. Set the intention you have a date and time you are going to be "meeting them."

You could get a picture of them or maybe one of their favorite things and have it near. Light a candle if you would like. Grab a journal in case you choose to write anything down.

When the day and time comes, find a spot you won't be disturbed and can be in the memory for as long as you'd like.

Clear your mind of anything else going on in your life. Close your eyes and start remembering. Bring in all of the things you remember about it.

- *Were you in nature?*

- *Was there music or any other sounds you remember playing or going on*

- *What were you doing?*

- *Was there a scent, a smell, an aroma that you can recall?*

- *What colors are you noticing?*

- *What are you seeing?*

- *Are you holding hands – was their hand soft or rough, cool or warm?*

- *What are you talking about, if anything?*

*The more details you add to this memory, the more you will feel as if you are there, in the memory again – because as the memory is being remembered – **you are there, reliving that scene.***

If you are thinking there will be more sadness when you open your eyes and come back to this reality, let that go. There may be initial sadness, and there will also be happiness and the memory you just recreated is another memory in your mind. It gets stronger the more times you replay it and remember it.

Journal if you would like. There may be emotions that come up or pieces of the memory that you had forgotten about that you start remembering.

You are spiritual beings having a human / physical experience. You wanted to come and learn things, see what this or that feels like. When you feel the separation from your loved ones (no matter the reason for the separation), really feel what that feeling is like. Then close your eyes and feel the connection. Feel the connection to your loved one, to nature, to the Divine and to yourself.

The connection is TRUTH, the separation is the ILLUSION.

~ Your Angels ~

connection with a loved one

Sue Broome

truth

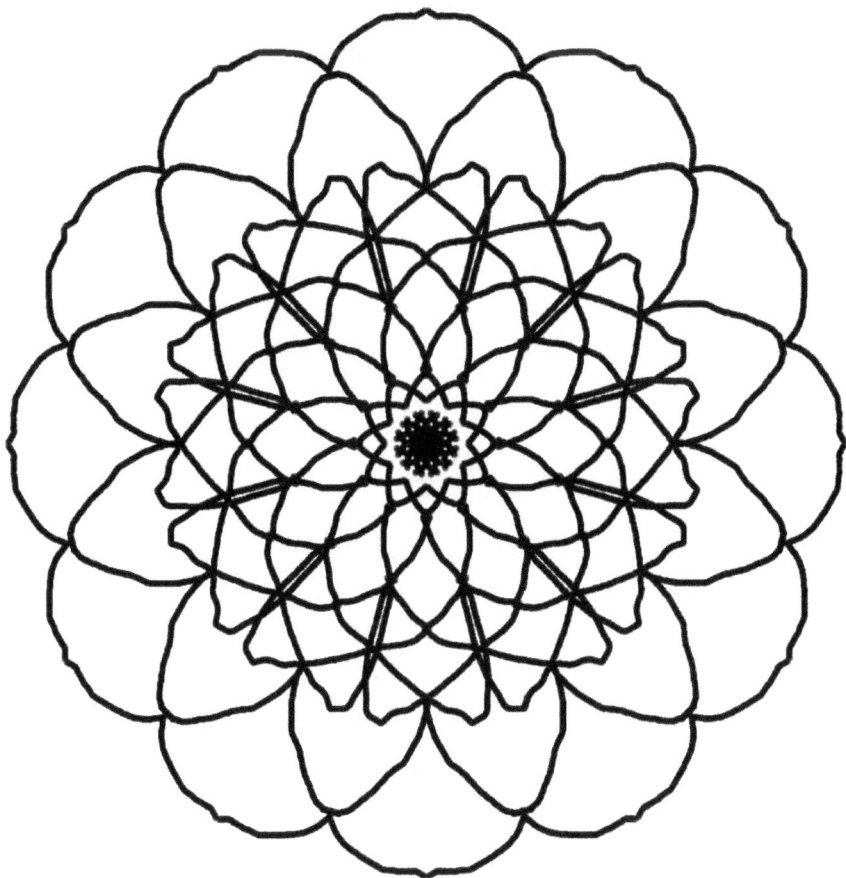

Sue Broome

Experience
a Boost of
Love Energy
and Appreciation

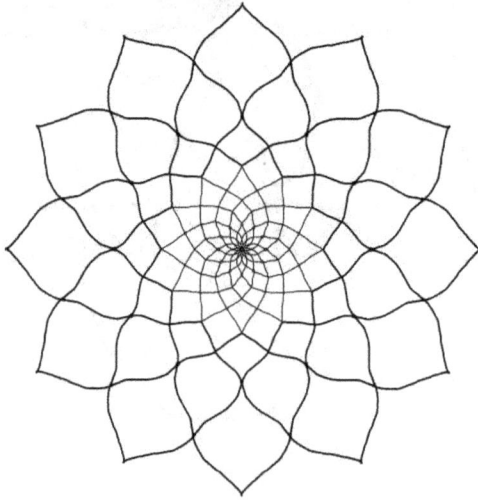

Dear Ones,

Today we would like you to experience, running your own energy:

- *Close your eyes and take a couple of deep breaths, in through the nose and out through the mouth.*

- *Imagine the love of the Divine as a white column of light coming from the top of your head, moving down through your torso and down into Mother Earth.*

- *Imagine the love of Mother Earth coming up and connecting with the love of the Divine.*

- *You can feel the energy and love moving up and down, not being able to tell where one begins or ends as it's now merged with you and there is no beginning or end.*

- *You can now ask a color to join or you can see what color(s) you may notice.*

- *Allow the loving energy to continue as long as you would like.*

- *When you are ready, thank the Divine, Mother Earth and yourself.*

- *Open your eyes when you are ready.*

This is something you can do anytime throughout your day for a quick boost of love, energy and appreciation.

~ Your Angels ~

Sue Broome

boost of love energy and appreciation

Sue Broome

appreciation

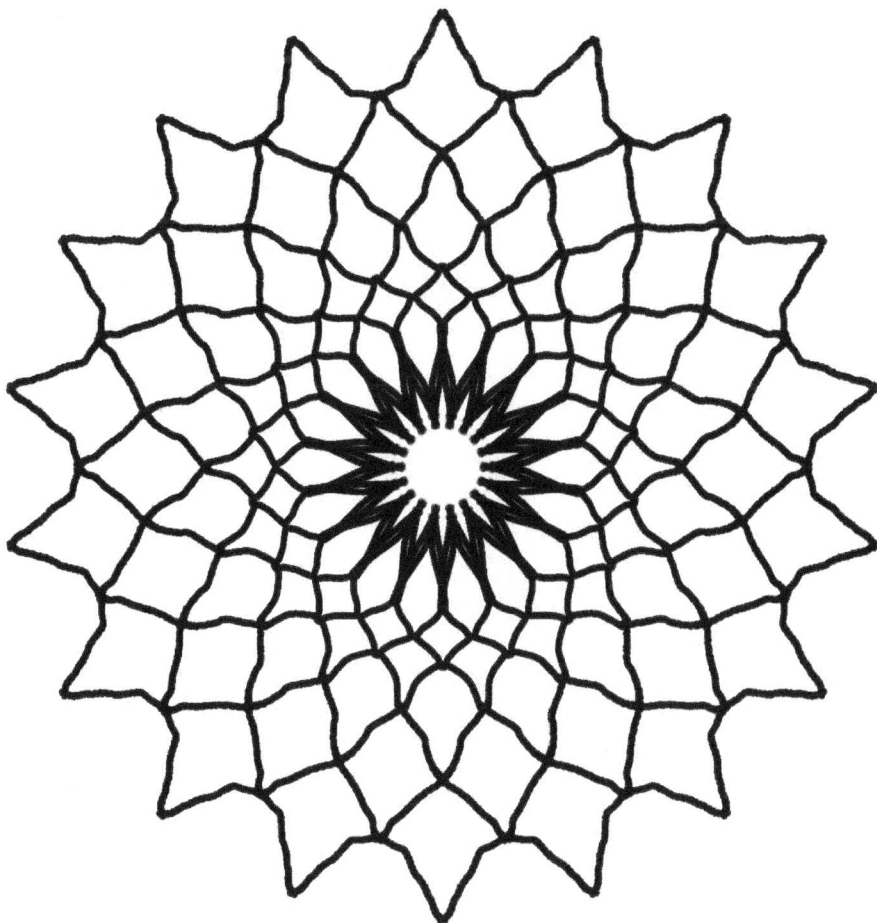

Sue Broome

Experience

the

Unraveling

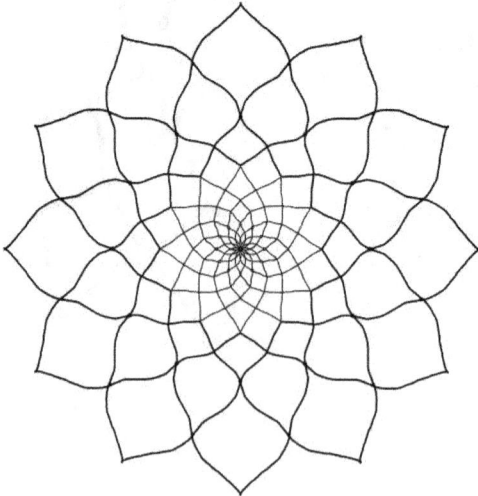

Dear Ones,

Today we speak of the unraveling occurring with many.

Your life is a series of experiences, beliefs, knowings, truths, perceptions, etc. You have all of these things that form who you are today, going on around you, with you sometimes, yet not always, being a part of it.

They cover you at times and mask who you truly are.

You get to a point, where unravelling begins. Getting to that point is different for everyone in how they get there, what may have happened to start and even how it progresses.

With the unraveling you may realize:

- *That wasn't my belief ~ I can choose to believe what I want*

- *That experience doesn't define me ~ it is something that happened to me and I can choose how I allow it to 'be' or 'not' in my life now*

- *My perceptions are different now ~ I am an adult looking at things with adult knowing and I can nurture the child who had the perceptions*

The unraveling is occurring not to scare you or ruin what or where you think you are. It is meant to reveal. With the unraveling, it brings you back to the Truth of you being a spiritual being, a spark of the Divine.

You can speed the unraveling up or slow it down or allow it to go at the speed it chooses. Whenever you feel things unraveling, no matter the speed, here is something you can do:

- *Sit quietly and close your eyes.*

- *Take several deep breaths.*

- *Feel the connection with the Divine strengthen with each breath you take.*

- *Allow the unraveling to occur. Notice as old beliefs fall away, or things you thought were true but now they seem to longer fit who you are becoming.*

- *Observe this as if it is happening to someone else.*

- *Acknowledge as each thing unravels and dissolves and transmutes to love.*

- *Realize it served you at another point in time.*

- *Thank it for what you may have learned from it.*

- *Allow this process to continue as long as you need, staying in the observer role.*

- *When you are ready, fill up with Divine love.*

- *Take a couple of deep breaths, grounding yourself and slowly coming back into your body.*

- *Open your eyes when you are ready.*

Notice how much lighter you feel. When you are feeling life is happening to you, is a good time to do this exercise.

~ Your Angels ~

unraveling

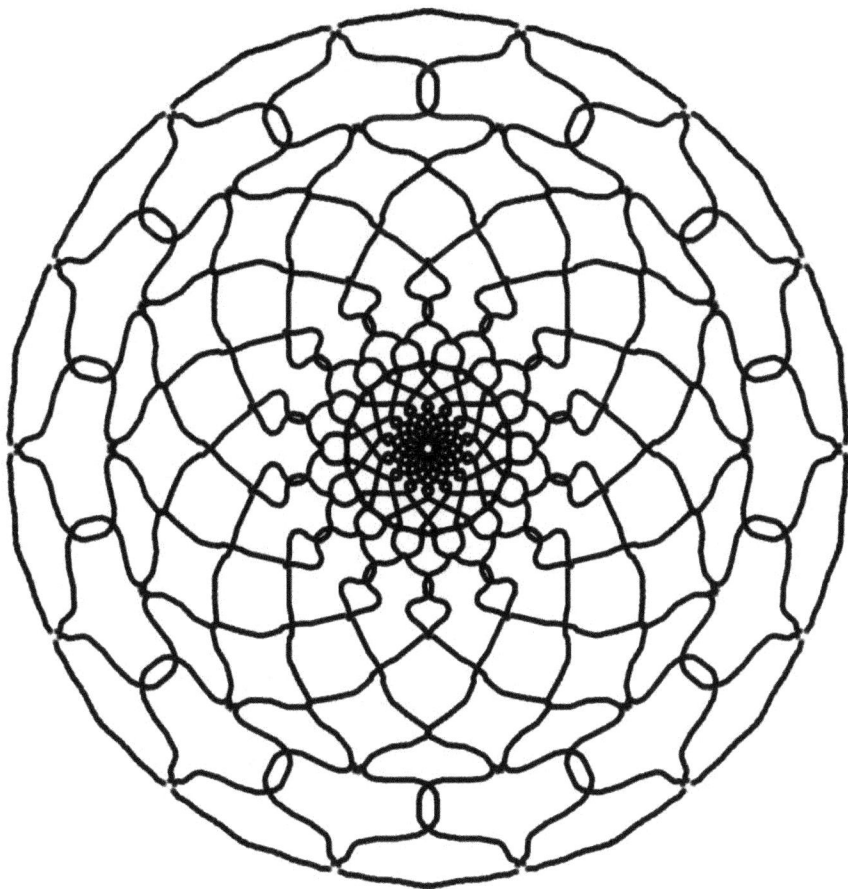

Sue Broome

Experience

Your

Light

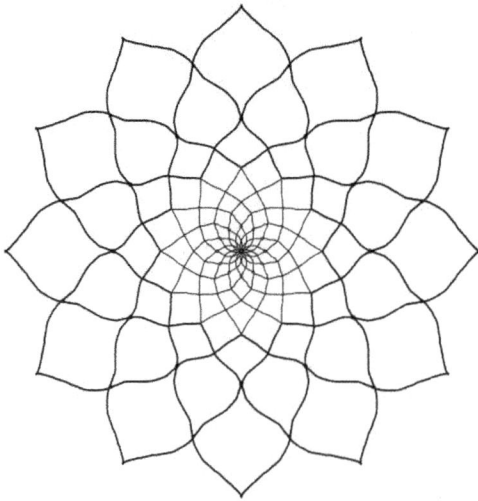

Dear Ones,

Today we speak of your beauty, your sparkle, your light, your love. We wish for you to see yourself as we see you.

If you can imagine or remember the most magnificent, the most brilliant, the most wonderful spirit you have ever known. Now multiply that feeling by 10x, by 100x, by 1000x and then some. That is how we see you.

You have such a beautiful light. You sparkle and you shine. You are not dull as some of you think of yourselves. Your life experiences bring out the brilliance within. It is not something to be hidden away.

You are right where you are supposed to be, shining your light and sharing who you are with those around you. You have a wisdom within. Sharing who you are, your inner light, helps others to recognize and see their inner light.

You are only responsible for your own light, shining it as bright as you possibly can. When you shine who you are it is shared with others. Shining your light is in:

- *The stories you tell*

- *The work you do*

- *The way you raise your children*

- *The way you are with strangers*

- *The way you are with the cashier at the grocery store*

- *The way you are — period*

Shine your light and allow the inner wisdom and beauty to sparkle and show. Recognize the light you are.

~ Your Angels ~

Sue Broome

your light

Sue Broome

The next few experiences (Experience the Angels' Love, I, II and III) are for feeling the Angels' love. They are similar yet have subtle differences. This is why the Angels decided to keep them all and this is what they have to say about it.

You may be wondering why we continue to speak on the same topic. It is because you all experience our love in different ways and we want to be able to reach as many of you as possible. We and many other beings of love and light, all of the highest vibration continue to send love to all inhabitants of Gaia. The more of you that can fully embrace this feeling of love, the more human consciousness expands. And as you the individual expands, it aids others in their expansion.

We are here to assist you in any way we can.

Sue Broome

Experience
the
Angels'
Love I

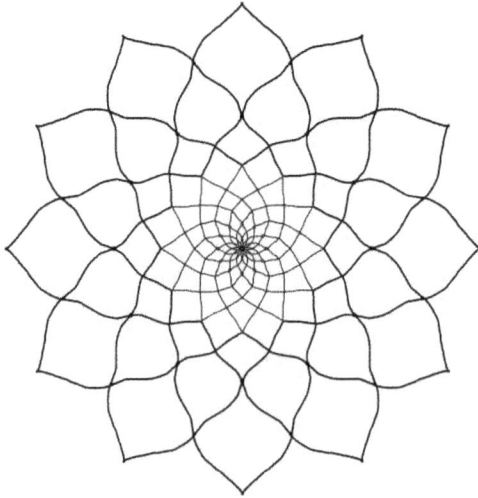

Dear Ones,

Today we would like you to experience our love we feel for you. Yes, this is truly an experience. You can read about it and then take the time to feel, to experience, to be in the loving energy.

- *Close your eyes and take several deep breaths.*

- *Feel your body relaxing into the chair you are sitting in.*

- *Feel any worries, any stresses just fall away as you sink more into you.*

- *Imagine we are sending you wave upon wave upon wave of love.*

- *You may see this similar to ripples in a pond.*

- *With each wave of energy, you feel more things wash away.*

- *And with each wave of energy you feel more and more a sense of peace wash over you.*

- *The feeling you may experience may be contentment, a knowingness, a remembering, a love you hadn't realized was there.*

- *Bask in this feeling as often and as long as you would like, knowing it is here for you at any moment of time.*

- *When you are ready, wiggle your toes, your fingers, come back into your body and open your eyes.*

We love you, we are here for you. We hope you could feel and experience our love for you.

~ Your Angels ~

Sue Broome

angels' love I

Sue Broome

Experience

the

Angels'

Love II

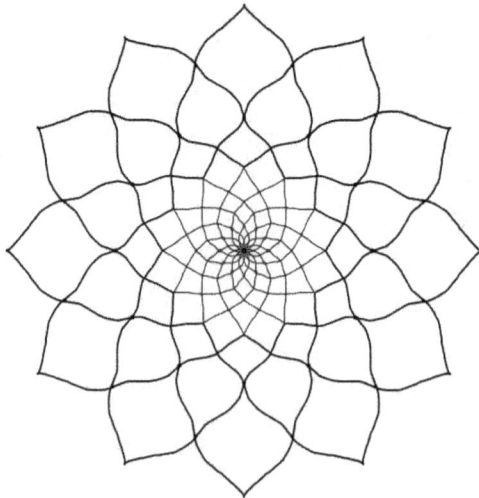

Dear Ones,

We are here to remind you that you are never alone. There are many who are going through things where they feel there is nowhere to turn. We are always with you.

- *When you feel sad, feel our love and our light wrap around you in a blanket filled with love.*

- *When you feel happy, feel our excitement for you and feel us jumping up and down right along with you.*

- *When you feel angry, know that we are here, gently lifting your vibration so the anger passes through quickly and is released and transmuted to love.*

- *When you feel grief over the loss of a friend or family member, or the loss of a job, know that we are here with you, feeling this loss right along with you. We are gently nudging you to look at all of the wonderful things you experienced about your friend or family member, or about the place you worked. We are right there with you.*

The times you feel most alone — we want you to know we are here with you. We surround you with love and light. We may send you a feather or another sign so you'll know we are near. We may send you the scent of your favorite flower to let you know we're here.

You are loved. You are never alone. We are here.

~ Your Angels ~

Sue Broome

angels' love II

Sue Broome

Experience the Angels' Love III

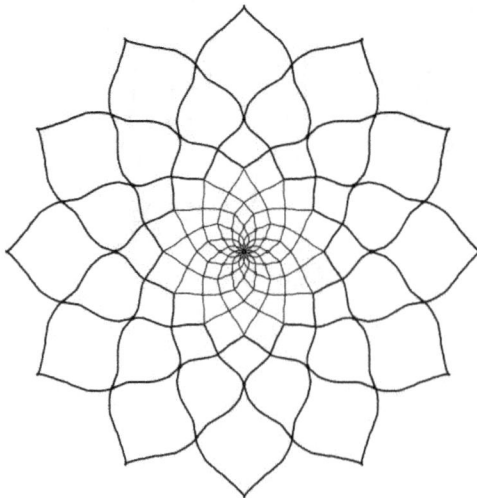

Dear Ones,

Today we speak of the love we are sending to you. We have spoken of this in other ways. Today we offer another way of experiencing our love.

Imagine you are sitting or lying down in the most comfortable chair or bed possible. You can feel every part of your being; your entire body relaxes.

- *You feel your muscles release any tensions they may hold.*

- *You feel your thoughts easily drift away.*

- *You feel any worries have now turned into wonder and are released.*

- *You feel your emotions turn to bliss.*

- *You know there is nothing that needs to be done or to think about at this particular moment in time.*

In this state of bliss, you realize there is a warmth surrounding you, as if it is holding you, supporting you. It is so soft it is as if you are on a pillow made of a cloud. Every part of your being feels loved, supported, nurtured and enveloped in love.

Stay in this loving space of bliss for as long as you would like. Know this is our way of loving you, of helping you to "feel" our love, our support. It is our way for you to know we are here.

Every night as you are drifting off to sleep, take a few minutes to imagine this and know we love you.

~ Your Angels ~

Sue Broome

angels' love III

Sue Broome

Experience

the

Love

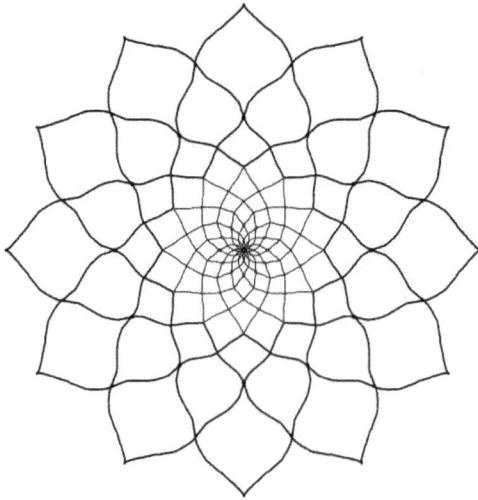

Dear Ones,

Today we speak of love. Love is all around you, love is within you, love is everywhere. We have spoken of love before. It is important you feel love, not just "think" love.

Love is the answer everyone is searching for. Accepting yourself and your life, loving yourself and who you are, feeling the love of the Divine and allowing it to emanate through you to others.

They will look at you and think "I would like some of what you have." They will feel the love though they may not be able to articulate it. If they are not ready to accept the love and the light you are, they may become frightened, angry, frustrated or annoyed and retreat or walk away.

You are here to be you. to be love, to experience love. You are here to allow love from the Divine.

Loving yourself is where it starts. We have stated this before. This is important for you to feel, to share with others. This message is for all who are ready to hear.

- *Close your eyes and feel into a time when you were surrounded by love, whether it was another person or an animal friend.*

- *Feel your love for them and feel their love for you.*

- *Be in that moment, in that feeling of love.*

- *Allow it to penetrate your cells, your very core.*

- *Place your hands on your heart and continue to feel the loving energy.*

- *Stay with this feeling as long as you can.*

- *When you are ready, open your eyes.*

Throughout your day, if you would like a boost of this wonderful and loving energy, place one or both hands on your heart. You will feel it.

Sue Broome

~ Your Angels ~

love

Sue Broome

Experience

Love

Flowing

to You

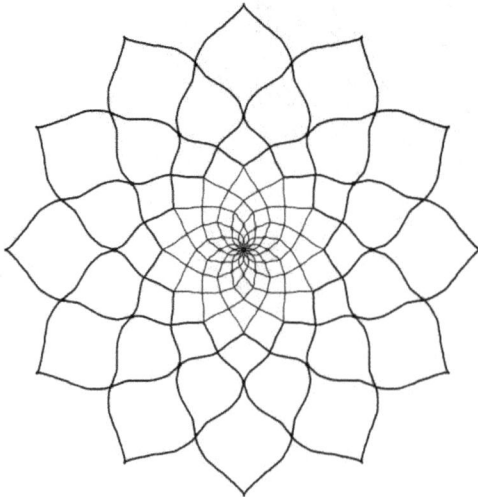

Dear Ones,

Allow your body, your cells, your heart and your mind to be filled with love. You do not need to 'do' anything. Sit back and accept love to flow in and through you.

So many times, you are having to do the tasks on your list or the things others are asking of you. This is something different Dear Ones.

Allow. No need to do a task, no need to do anything. Allow and accept.

- *Find a location where you will not be disturbed.*

- *Close your eyes.*

- *Take several deep breaths, in through the nose, hold, out through the mouth — to a count of four for each (a count of four as you breathe in, hold for a count of four, blow out for a count of four and wait for a count of four.) Do this four times.*

- *Allow the feeling of love to come in through your crown chakra (the top of your head.) You may imagine it as a color, as a white light, as sparkly — whatever works for you.*

- *Allow the feeling to come in through your crown and move slowly down through every inch, every cell of your body.*

- *Allow the feeling of love from the Divine to flow out through your feet down into Mother Earth. This may feel like a wonderful waterfall of energy come into the top of your head, flow through your body, leaving behind love, light, healing, calm, peace and joy, and as it flows out through your feet, all of the love, light, healing, calm, peace and joy, is flowing into Mother Earth.*

- *When you are ready, take another breath or two, integrating all of this loving energy into your being.*

- *Open your eyes when you are ready.*

You may have another experience. Everyone will have their own unique experience, each time.

~ Your Angels ~

love flowing to you

Sue Broome

Experience

the

Stillness

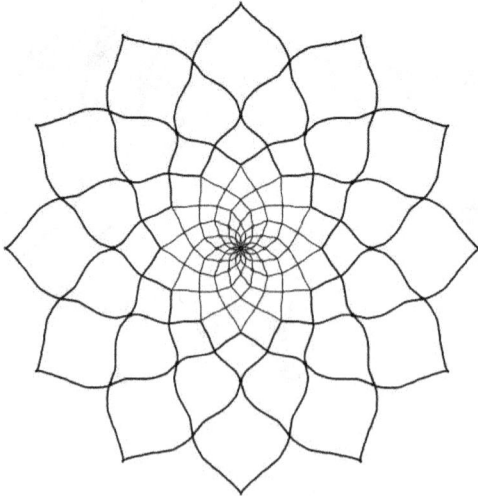

Dear Ones,

Today we speak of going into the stillness.

It may not be stillness around you. In fact, your world may be chaotic with a lot going on. This is not the stillness we speak of.

We are speaking of no matter where you may be, you can easily find the stillness within. The stillness allows you to hear your own breath and feel your own heartbeat. This stillness allows you to hear or feels your blood moving through your veins.

This stillness also allows you to "see" what you normally may not notice and to "hear" what you may not have heard before.

This stillness is always there and at times you may need to go searching it out. It is easy enough to find if you know where to look, if you know how to get there.

- *Sit quietly, eyes closed or open is up to you (if open, allow them to get soft so they aren't focusing on anything specific.)*

- *Notice your breathing without changing it, just notice.*

- *The more still you get, you'll begin to notice — sounds, sights, flashes of light. Allow them to just be, without looking to change them or focus on them.*

- *Now start to focus on the spaces between — between any noise, between your breath, between the words, between the pictures and allow it to expand.*

- *You'll start to feel the calm, the peace, the stillness.*

- *When you find the stillness within, acknowledge it, embrace it, thank it and feel it expand within and without.*

- *When you are ready, open your eyes.*

You will notice a much calmer you than when you began.

Sue Broome

~ Your Angels ~

stillness

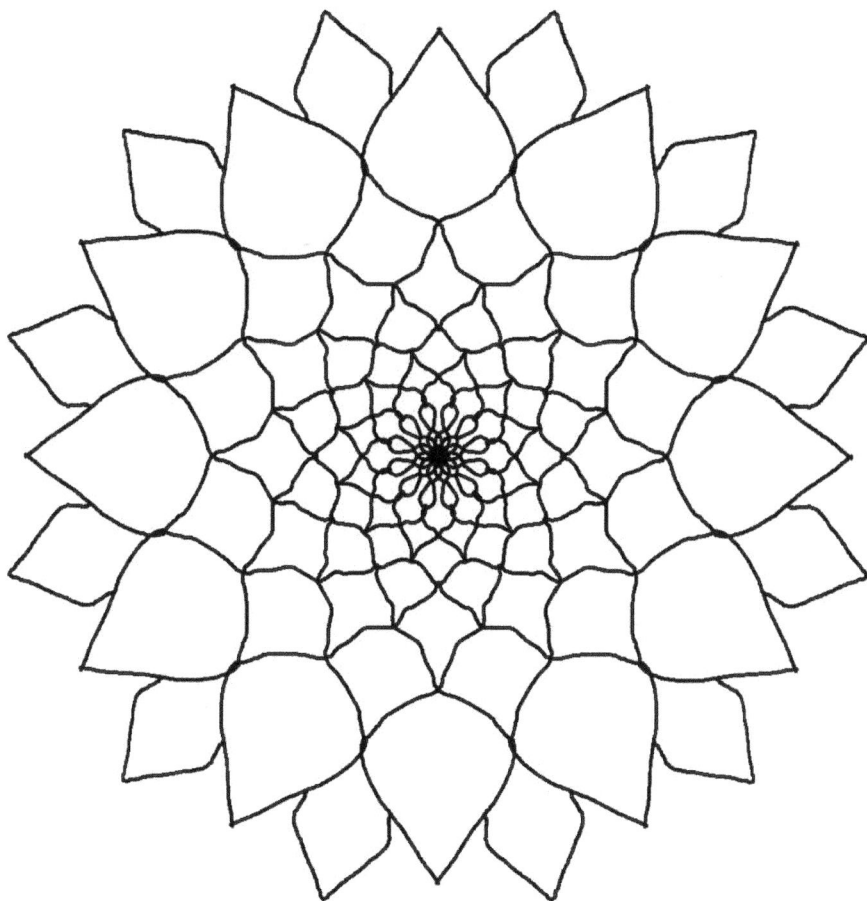

Sue Broome

Experience

the

Calm

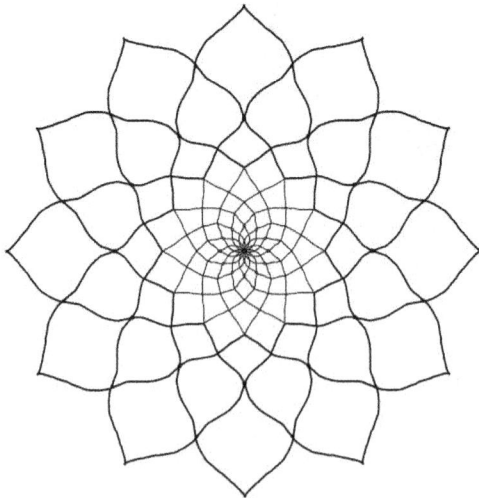

Dear Ones,

Today we wish to help on the days things feel out of control.

- *Close your eyes and focus on your breath, bringing it to a steady in and a steady out.*

- *Notice the swirls of energy all around you, like waves in an ocean. Notice how high they go, how far reaching they are.*

- *Now imagine and notice the waves falling upon a sandy beach. They may come in strong but they fall away and dissipate as soon as they come onto the shoreline.*

- *Notice as the water hits the shoreline, much of it disappears into the sand, being soaked up like a sponge.*

- *Notice as the water slowly goes back out to sea.*

- *Focus your attention on the calming of the shoreline as the wave almost falls into the sand and disappears.*

- *Allow the calming of the waves, shifting, changing and disappearing, to continue to be your focus.*

- *Stay here as long as you would like and come back often.*

~ Your Angels ~

Sue Broome

calm

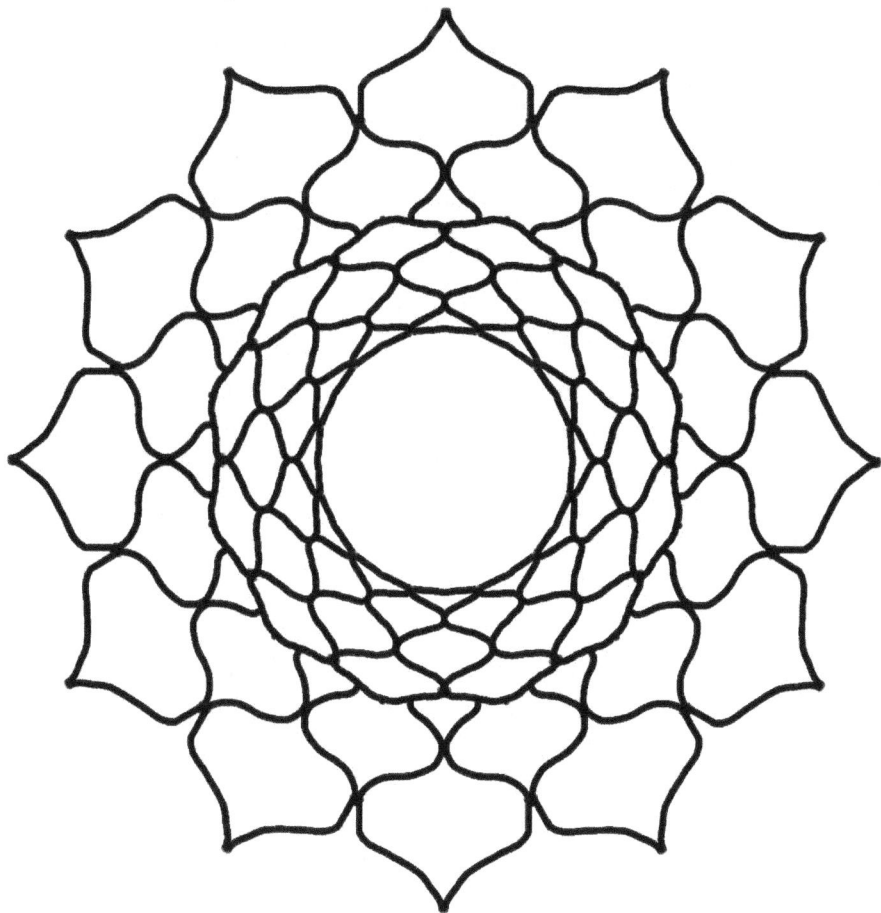

About the Author

Sue Broome is a gifted intuitive healer and spiritual teacher. She works with the Divine and Angels in guiding others on their spiritual healing journey. She shares tools of empowerment in each session and is available for healings and readings which offer guidance from the Angels.

Sue is a host with International Angels Network. *Angel Talk with Sue* is available Wednesdays at 9pm ET. This allows her to reach a global audience.

She loves sharing with others how to connect with their loved ones through her book, *Signs From Your Loved Ones* and her courses. *Memories Shared with your Loved Ones* and *Channel Writing with Mom* are currently available.

Sue works with groups, individuals in private sessions and continues to create online courses and products. Sessions are available through phone, email or Skype. She created *The Desert Speaks* oracle deck which can be used for inspiration and readings. It is available on her website.

Enjoy Healing Tools From the Angels, a gift, a PDF to work with the Angels at https://empowerment4you.com/angel-talk-with-sue

Contact info:

Email: su.broome@gmail.com

Website: Empowerment4You.com

Online training: Sue-Broome.Teachable.com

Facebook: facebook.com/Empowerment4You/

Instagram: @SueBroome44

YouTube Channel: bit.ly/SueBroomeYouTube

Radio: InternationalAngelsNetwork.com/Sue

www.ingramcontent.com/pod-product-compliance
Lightning Source LLC
Chambersburg PA
CBHW052114090426
42741CB00009B/1799